ON OLD A
(De Senectute)

Marcus Tullius Cicero

Translated by Andrew P. Peabody.
Initially published in 1887.

Table of Contents

INTRODUCTION. 3

ATTICUS. 13

CATO. 18

LAELIUS. 25

SCIPIO. 27

CICERO DE SENECTUTE. 29

INTRODUCTION.

After the death of Julius Caesar, and before the conflict
with Antony, Cicero spent two years in retirement,
principally at his Tusculan villa. It was the most fruitful
season of his life, as regards philosophy. To this period
(B. C. 45 or 44) the authorship of the De Senectute is
commonly assigned. In his De Divinatione, in
enumerating his philosophical works, he speaks of this
treatise on Old Age as "lately thrown in among them,"[1]
and as meriting a place in the list. In the De Amicitia,
dedicated also to Atticus, he says: "In the Cato Major,
the book on Old Age inscribed to you, I introduced the
aged Cato as leading in the discussion, because no
person seemed better fitted to speak on the subject than
one who both had been an old man so long, and in old
age had still maintained his preeminence. . . . . In
reading that book of mine, I am sometimes so moved
that it seems to me as if, not I, but Cato were talking. . .
. . I then wrote about old age, as an old man to an old
man."[1] Again, Laelius, who is the chief speaker in the
De Amicitia, is introduced as saying, "Old age is not
burdensome, as I remember hearing Cato say in a
conversation with me and Scipio, the year before he
died." Cicero repeatedly refers to this book in his
Letters to Atticus. In the stress of apprehension about
Antony's plans and movements he writes: "I ought to
read very often the Cato Major which I sent to you; for
old age is making me more bitter. Everything puts me
out of temper." At a later time he writes, "By saying
that O Tite, si quid ego,[2] delights you more and more,
you increase my readiness to write." And again, "I
rejoice that O Tite[2] is doing you good."

3

In his philosophical and ethical writings, Cicero lays no claim to originality; nor, indeed, did the Romans of his age, or even of a much later time, regard themes of this kind as properly their own. Philosophy was an exotic which it was glory enough for them to prize and cultivate. This fame appertains pre-eminently to Cicero, equally for his comprehensive scholarship, for his keenness of critical discernment, and for his generous eclecticism. Were it not for his explicit statement, we might not learn from his writings to what sect he accounted himself as belonging. Though he disclaimed the Stoic school, he evidently felt a strong gravitation toward it, and we could ask for no better expositor of its doctrines than we find in him. Indeed, I can discover no reason for his adherence to the New Academy, except the liberty which it left to its disciples to doubt its own dogmas, and to acknowledge a certain measure of probability in the dogmas of other schools.

In this treatise Cicero doubtless borrowed something from Aristo of Chios, a Stoic, to whose work on Old Age — no longer extant — he refers, and he quotes largely from Xenophon and Plato. At the same time, thick-sown tokens of profound conviction and deep feeling show that the work, if not shaped from his experience, was the genuine utterance of his aspirations. What had been his life was forever closed.1 He was weary and sad. His home was desolate, and could never again be otherwise. His daughter — dearer to him than any other human being had ever been — had recently died, and he had still more recently repudiated her young step-mother for lack of sympathy with him in his sorrow. His only son was giving him great solicitude and grief by his waywardness and profligacy. The republic to which he had consecrated his warm devotion and loyal service had ceased to be, and gave faint hope of renewed vitality. The Senate-house, the popular assembly, and the courts were closed for him, and might never be reopened. He had courted publicity, and had delighted in office, leadership, and influence; but there was now little likelihood that any party that might come into power would replace him, where he felt that he had a right to be, among the guiding and controlling spirits of his time.

Old age with him is just beginning, and it may last long. He is conscious of no failure in bodily or mental vigor, — in the capacity of work or of enjoyment. Yet in all that had contributed to his fame and his happiness, he has passed the culminating point; he is on the westward declivity of his life-way; decrease and decline are inevitable. But shall he succumb to the inevitable in sullen despondency, or shall he explore its resources for a contented and enjoyable life, and put them to the test of experience? He chooses the latter alternative, and it is not as the mere rehearsal of what he has read in Greek books, but with the glow of fresh discovery, and in the spirit of one who is mapping out the ground of which he means to take possession, that he describes what old age has been, what it may still be, and what he yearns to make it for himself. He grows strong, cheerful, and hopeful as he writes, and in coming times of distress and peril he unrolls this little volume for his own support and consolation.

In imitation of the Platonic pattern, followed by him in several previous treatises, he adopts the form of dialogue; but after the interchange of a few sentences the dialogue becomes monologue, and Cato talks on without interruption to the end. Cato is chosen as the principal interlocutor, because he was the typical old man of Roman history, having probably retained his

5

foremost place in the public eye, and his oratorical power in the Senate and at the bar, to a later age than any other person on record. In his part in this dialogue there is a singular commingling of fact, truth, and myth. The actual details of his life are gracefully interwreathed with the discussion, and the incidental notices of his elders and coevals are precisely such as might have fallen from his lips had he been of a more genial temperament. There is dramatic truth, too, in Cato's senile way of talking, with the garrulity, repetition, prolixity, and occasional confusion of names, to which old men are liable, and in which Cicero merges his own precision and accuracy in the character which for the time he assumes. But as regards the kindly, the aesthetic, and the spiritual traits that make this work so very charming, its Cato is a mythical creation, utterly unlike the coarse, hard, stern, crabbed ex-Censor, who was guiltless equally of taste and of sentiment.

Cicero's reasoning in this treatise is based, in great part, on what old age may be, rather than on what it generally is; and yet I cannot but believe that, were its cautions heeded, its advice followed, and its spirit inbreathed, the number of those who find in the weight of many years no heavy burden would be largely multiplied. Yet there would remain not a few cases of hopeless inanity and helpless suffering. We are here told, and with truth, that it is often the follies and sins of early life that embitter the declining years; yet infirmity sometimes overtakes lives that have been blameless and exemplary, nor does the strictest hygienic regimen always arrest the failure of body and of mind. Undoubtedly the worst thing that an old man can do is to cease from labor and to cast off responsibility. The powers suffered to repose lapse from inaction into inability; while they will in most cases continue to meet the drafts made upon them, if those drafts recur with wonted frequency and urgency. Yet there is always danger that, as in the case of the Archbishop in Gil Blas, the old man who insists on doing his full tale of work will be mistaken in thinking that undiminished quantity implies unimpaired quality.

But apart from the continued life-work, Cicero indicates resources of old age which are as genuine and as precious now as they were two thousand years ago. While the zest of highly seasoned convivial enjoyment, especially of such as abuts upon the disputed border-ground between sobriety and excess, is exhaled, there is fully as much to be enjoyed in society as in earlier years. Perhaps even more; for as friends grow few, those that remain are all the dearer, and in the company of those in early or middle life, the old man finds himself an eager learner as to the rapidly fleeting present, and imagines himself a not unwelcome teacher as to what deserves commemoration in the obsolescent and outgrown past. The tokens of deference and honor uniformly rendered in society to old age that has not forfeited its title to respect are a source of pleasure. They are, indeed, in great part, conventional; but for this very reason they only mean and express the more, inasmuch as they betoken, not individual feeling, but the general sentiment of regard and reverence for those whose long life-record is unblotted.

Rural pursuits and recreations, also, as Cicero says, are of incalculable worth to the aged. The love of nature increases with added years. In the outward universe there is an infinity of beauty and of loveliness. The Creator englobes his own attributes in all his works. What we get from them is finite, solely because the taste and feeling that apprehend them are finite. But our receptivity grows with the growth of character, and our revenue of delight from field and garden, orchard and forest, brook and stream, sunset clouds and star-gemmed skies, is in full proportion to our receptivity, and is never so rich and so gladdening as in the later years of life. Cicero evidently felt this. There is hardly anything in all his works so beautiful as the sections of this treatise in which he describes the growth of the corn and the vine, and the simple joys of a country home. Indeed, this is almost a unique passage. The literature of nature is, for the most part, of modern birth. The classic writers give now and then, in a single phrase or sentence, a vivid word-picture of scenery or of some phenomenon in the outward world; but they seldom dwell on such themes. Even pastoral poetry sings of the flocks and their keepers, rather than of their material surroundings. But here we have proof that Cicero had grown into an appreciation of the wealth of beauty lying around his villa, far beyond what would have been possible for him when he sought its quiet as a refuge from the turmoil and conflicts of his more active days.

Cicero is right, too, in regarding the presence of old men in the state as essential to its safety and well-being. True, their office is, for the most part, that of brakemen; but on a roadway never smooth, and passing over frequent declivities, this duty often demands more strength and skill than are required to light the fires and run the engine. It is only by a conservatism both wise and firm that progress can be made continuous and reform permanent. Nor is there any imminent probability that old age will furnish a larger array of conservative force than the world needs. If in the advancement of physical and moral hygiene the time should come when the hoary head shall be in due season the normal crown of every man, and, according to the Hebrew hyperbole, "the child shall die an hundred years old," society will have attained a summit-level at which there will be need neither of engineers nor of brakemen.

Meanwhile, it is well for mankind that old men are so few. Were they more numerous, and at the same time worthy to retain the confidence of their fellow-men, the young would lack the exercise and discipline of their powers which alone could fit them for an honorable and useful old age. Death oils all the wheels of life. It is always throwing heavy responsibility on those who do not seek it, but accept it as a necessity, and gird themselves to bear it faithfully and nobly. As in a well-trained army the reserved forces rush in to fill the places of the fallen, so in the battle of life the ranks of the dying are recruited by those who are biding their time. Death is the ripener of manly force and efficient virtue, which would droop under the dense shadow of thoroughly matured and still active service, but are stimulated into full vitality and working power as the spaces around them are made void. The very bereavements which are most dreaded and deplored as utterly irreparable, are the most certain to be repaired, and often by those who before neither knew themselves nor were known to be capable of such momentous charge and duty. Elijah wears his mantle till he goes to heaven, and there is no other on earth like it; but when he ascends he drops the mantle, and his spirit enters into the man who picks it up. Death is, indeed, looked upon as a calamity by many whose faith should have taught them better. The death which closes an undevout and worthless life may well be dreaded; yet even in such a case continued life is perhaps to be still more dreaded.

But in the order designed by Infinite Wisdom, and destined to progressive and ultimate establishment, death bears a supremely beneficent part, and is an event only to be welcomed in its appointed season by him who has brought his own life into conformity with the Divine order.

But death can be regarded with complacency only when it is looked upon, — as Cicero represents it, — as not an end, but a way, — as not a ceasing to live, but a beginning to live. The jubilant strains in which the assurance of immortality is here voiced are hardly surpassed in grandeur by St. Paul's words of triumph when the crown of martyrdom hung close within his reach. Yet there is a difference. Cicero's faith transcended, and in great part created, his reasons for it, and it failed him in the very crises in which he most needed it; St. Paul "knew in whom he had believed," and his faith was sightlike when death seemed nearest. It is of no little worth to us that Socrates and Plato, Cicero and Plutarch, felt so intensely the pulse-beat of the undying life within. Of inestimably greater evidential value is it, that he whose peerless beauty of holiness made his humanity divine ever spoke of the eternal life as the one reality of human being. But there are for us emergencies of sore need and of heavy trial, times when we go down to the margin of the death-river with those dear to us as our own souls, critical moments when we ourselves are passing under the shadow of death; and at such seasons we can rest on no reasoning, we can be satisfied with no unbuttressed testimony; but our faith can repose in undoubting security on the broken sepulchre, on the risen Saviour, on those words spoken for all time, "Because I live, ye shall live also."

ATTICUS.

Titus Pomponius, as he was originally named, on his adoption by his uncle prefixed that uncle's name, Quintus Caecilius, to his own, and subsequently, in consequence of his long residence in Athens, assumed, or received and accepted, the surname of Atticus, by which he is known in history. He was born in Rome, 109 B. C., and was Cicero's senior by three years. He belonged to an old Equestrian family, not eminent, but of high respectability. His father was a man of culture and of literary tastes, and gave his son a liberal education. The civil war between the factions of Marius and Sulla broke out in the son's early manhood, and he hardly escaped being a victim of Sulla's proscription. He determined to insure safety by voluntary exile, and, his father being dead, he betook himself with the movable portion of his ample patrimony to Athens, where he lived for twenty years.

He called himself an Epicurean, and, though not deeply versed in philosophy, he probably realized more nearly than any man whose history we know the ethical ideal of Epicurus himself. Supremely, but judiciously selfish; covetous of pleasure, yet with an aesthetic sense which found pleasure only in things decent, tasteful, and becoming; a persistent and loyal friend, so far as friendship demanded neither conflict nor sacrifice; sedulously avoiding pain, annoyance, and trouble; plucking roses all along his lifeway so carefully as never to incur a thorn-prick, — he must have derived as large a revenue of enjoyment from his seventy-seven years in this world as ever accrued to any man whose aims were all self-centred and self-terminated.

He was fond of money, frugal while elegant in his mode of living, with no vices so far as we know, certainly with no costly vices. He was married only late in life, and had but one child to provide for. His uncle — a usurer of ignoble reputation — left him an estate five times as large as that received from his father. This he increased by the remunerative purchase of extensive tracts of land in Epeirus and elsewhere, by loans to individuals, corporations, and cities, by traffic in slaves and gladiators, and, as a publisher, by multiplying, for high prices, through the numerous copyists whom he owned, transcripts of Cicero's works and of other writings of friends who sought to reach the public by his agency. At the same time, he made a judicious investment of charities far within his income, in loans without interest and public benefactions to the city of Athens, in loans and gifts to those within the circle of his intimacy, and in gratuities to persons straitened or suffering through stress of political convulsions and perils.

He belonged, by sympathy and in his private correspondence, to the Marian, and then to the Pompeian party, and had a strong antipathy to the course and policy of Julius Caesar, his race and kind; but he publicly identified himself with no party, refrained from political activity of every sort, and refused contributions in aid even of movements that had his full approval and his best wishes. He was always ready to relieve the distressed members of both and of all parties. He held friendly relations equally with Julius Caesar and Pompey, Cassius and Antony, Brutus and Caesar Augustus.

He had the most winning and attractive manners, a voice of rare sweetness and melody, and conversational powers unsurpassed, if equalled, by any man of his time. He was hospitable, yet without extravagance or ostentation, and his entertainments, first in Athens, and then in Rome, were remarkable as reunions of all that there was of learning, genius, wit, and grace. He loved to maintain peaceful and harmonious relations among his wonted guests, and was persevering in his endeavors to reconcile differences, soothe jealousies, and prevent rivals from becoming enemies. It was wholly due to their common friend and host that Cicero and Hortensius, as alike candidates for the palm of eloquence, preserved at least the show of friendship.

Atticus was also a man of large and varied learning, was equally versed in Greek and in Roman literature, and used either tongue in speech and in writing as if he had never known any other. He was a thorough grammarian and a careful critic. His friends were in the habit of sending their works to him for a last revision, and it is by no means improbable that some of the delicate touches of Cicero's rhetoric may be due to his consummate taste and skill. He was himself an author, and wrote among other things an epitome of Roman history from the earliest time to his own. He was a ready and fluent letter-writer. But none of his writings are extant, except such few scraps of his epistles as are preserved in Cicero's answers to them.

The friendship between Cicero and Atticus began in their early boyhood. When Cicero first went to Athens — shortly after his defence of Roscius, and not improbably to escape the vengeance of Sulla — he found Atticus already established there, and for six months they, with Cicero's brother Quintus, who married the sister of Atticus, were constantly associated in study and in recreation. From that time Atticus was

Cicero's closest and dearest friend, entering with the most vivid interest into all his plans and pursuits, lending him money, advising him in business, taking care of his property during his absences, and rendering counsel and aid in connection with the successive divorces of Terentia and Publilia. The correspondence between them now extant commenced only three years before Atticus returned to Rome, though it is hardly possible that they should not have exchanged letters previously. On Cicero's side the epistles are of the most familiar character, giving us a minute narrative of incident, occupation, thought, and sentiment, day by day, and furnishing more ample and more authentic materials for his biography than are derived from all other sources. They include equally such references to the details of the life of Atticus, and to all his peculiarities of habit, opinion, and taste, that we feel hardly less intimately acquainted with him than with his illustrious correspondent. He became to Cicero as another self, an admirer of his genius, a participant in all his ambitions, and in many matters of practical life by far the wiser of the two. That he knew the worth, prized the privilege, and undoubtedly anticipated the enduring fame of such a friendship, is the best title that remains on record to the place which he would have claimed in the list of genuine philosophers.

CATO.

Marcus Porcius Cato Censorius was born at Tusculum in Latium, probably B. C. 234, and died at the age of at least eighty-five years. Livy and Plutarch both say that he passed his ninetieth year. He was of plebeian birth, and the founder of his own illustrious family. Porcius was the family name, and Cato was a name either given to him in childhood with foresight of his shrewdness and practical wisdom, or else bestowed on him and accepted by him after his peculiar traits of character were well known and distinctly recognized. It denotes wisdom of an entirely terrestrial, and even feline type, and is on the whole more appropriate to him than the surname Sapiens, which attached itself to him in his later years. He had great virtues, but defects as great. In not one of the beatitudes in the Sermon on the Mount could he have claimed a part, nor would he have deigned to claim it, unless, in the almost numberless suits at law in which he was his own advocate, he might have regarded himself as "persecuted for righteousness' sake." He was rigidly truthful, sternly and ferociously upright, intensely courageous, and devotedly patriotic, — kind, too, to his wives and children. But he was mean and miserly, an exacting and tyrannical master, an implacable enemy, and his lower appetites were not governed by principle, but kept in check only so far as prudence required. He probably seemed a better man in Cicero's time than in his own, and this for two reasons; namely, that his peculiar virtues had almost died out of the Roman commonwealth, and that, when a man transmits to posterity any valid title to fame, time enhances his merits and extenuates his faults, so that the generation which "builds the sepulchres of the prophets" always idealizes the busts that surmount them.

As regards versatility of endowment, number and diversity of official trusts, ability and faithfulness as a servant of the public, and influence — unspent by death — over the Senate and the people, Cato had no equal in the history of Rome. The impress of his life and character on the ages that looked back on his career from the interval of centuries, may best be seen from Livy's panegyric, of which we give a literal translation. After enumerating the long list of competitors for the office of Censor, he says: —

"Marcus Porcius stood in the canvass far before all the patricians and plebeians of the most noble families. In this man there was so great force of mind and genius, that, whatever might have been his position by birth, he seemed destined to be the artificer of his own fortune. He lacked no skill in the management of either private or public interests. He was equally versed in the affairs of the city and of the country. Some have attained the highest honors by virtue of legal science, some by eloquence, some by military fame; he had a genius so capable of excelling in all, that whatever he had in hand you would say that he was expressly born for it. In war he was the bravest of soldiers, renowned in many signal conflicts; after he rose to high honors, a consummate general; in peace, if you asked legal advice, the wisest of counsellors; if you had a cause to be argued, the most eloquent of advocates. Nor was he one whose fame as an orator, flourishing while he lived, left no memorial of itself behind him. His eloquence still lives, consecrated by writings of every description. There are extant many of his speeches for himself, and for others, and against others; for he harassed his opponents equally by accusing them and by pleading his own cause. An excessive number of enmities were cherished against him, and cherished by him; nor was it easy to say whether the nobles were the more earnest to put him down, or he to annoy them. He was, undoubtedly, of a harsh temper, and of a bitter and an inordinately free tongue, but of a soul unconquered by sensual appetites,

of rigid integrity, a despiser of adulation and of bribes.
In frugal living, in endurance of labor and of danger, he
was of an iron constitution of body and mind; nor could
old age, which enfeebles all things, break him. In his
eighty-sixth year he had a case in court, pleaded his own
cause, and continued to write, and in his ninetieth year
he brought Servius Galba to trial before the people."

Cato inherited a small farm in the Sabine territory,
where he spent his boyhood and such portions of his
subsequent life as were free from public service. Here
he lived with the utmost simplicity, worked on his farm,
and associated on familiar terms with his rustic
neighbors. At the age of seventeen he made his first
campaign as a soldier, and three years later reached the
dignity of a military Tribune under Fabius Maximus,
whose friendship he enjoyed. B. C. 205, he went to Sicily
as military Quaestor under the elder Africanus. In due
time he became Aedile, and the next year Praetor,
having Sardinia for his province, with a considerable
military command. In this office he renounced the
wonted pomp of his predecessors, walked on his
circuits, cut down to the lowest point all public
expenses, waged war against usury, and visited usurers
with condign punishment. Chosen Consul B. C. 195, he
sustained during his term of office the only signal defeat
in his whole career. Twenty years previously, in the
stress of the Punic war, a severe sumptuary law had
been passed, limiting the amount of gold which women
might possess, forbidding them to wear many-colored
garments, and prohibiting their use of carriages for
short distances in the city. The women absolutely
mobbed the Senators, imploring the repeal of
restrictions no longer needed. Cato opposed them to the
last; but they by importunity won the day, and
celebrated their victory by a procession, in which they

made ample show of the late-proscribed finery. As soon as this domestic war was over, Cato set sail for his allotted province, Hither Spain (Hispania Citerior). Here there were rebel and recalcitrant tribes to be reduced to submission, and Cato in the conduct of this campaign displayed at once the highest military ability and the most wanton and savage cruelty. He was rewarded with a triumph; but returned to encounter the enmity of the elder Scipio Africanus, toward whom he had previously stood in unfriendly relations. He successfully defended himself against the charges urged against him, which seem to have related, in part at least, to the pecuniary administration of his province, in which Cato was able, by producing his accounts, to show himself, as in these matters he always was, not only above suspicion, but minutely exact, and as parsimonious in public office as he was in his own private affairs. He subsequently served under Glabrio, probably as Legatus, or lieutenant-general, in the war with Antiochus the Great, and the battle of Thermopylae, which crippled Antiochus, was brought to a successful issue confessedly by the prowess, energy, and strategic skill of Cato.

B. C. 184, Cato was chosen Censor, and applied himself at once with characteristic vigor and acrimony to the duties of his office. He made the most stringent provisions against luxury. He put the aqueducts, sewers, and other public works in order, and arrested all the modes in which public property had been perverted to private uses, such as the drawing off of water from the reservoirs for the special supply of houses and gardens. He brought farmers of the revenue and contractors of every class to strict account, and regulated all contracts by his own perhaps too low estimate of the actual worth of the work done or the service rendered. He degraded from the Senate and from their Equestrian privileges a very considerable number of men of previously high standing, most of them for grave and sufficient reasons, — some, it must be confessed, on very frivolous pretexts. He laid up by his censorial career a stock of enmities which lasted him for the rest of his life, during which he held no public office, but appeared constantly in the courts, in the Senate, and before the people, retaining to the last his clearness and vigor of intellect, and much of his oratorical power. He was during his lifetime prosecuted before the tribunals forty-four times, and failed of successful defence but once. He was still oftener a public accuser, and generally procured the conviction of the defendant. In the case of Servius Galba, recorded by Livy as his last, he lost the cause, though a righteous one, by the wonted resource of an appeal by weeping children to the pity of the judges.

Cato, though not a profligate or a sot, was not consistently pure nor uniformly temperate. He dealt with his slaves as with cattle, treating them as merchantable chattels, punishing them with wanton severity, and sometimes condemning them to death for trivial offences. His whole life must have been coarse, in many aspects even brutal, and the aesthetic faculty seems to have been entirely wanting in him.

Yet his literary culture must have been of a high order. He learned Greek in his old age, after despising the language and its writers during the whole of his earlier life. He was a friend and patron of the poet Ennius, and brought him to Rome, though manifestly without any generous provision for his subsistence; for Ennius led in Rome as poor and straitened a life as he could have left in Sardinia, where Cato found him. Of Cato's orations, letters, and great historical work, we have only fragments extant. His De Re Rustica exists, probably unchanged in substance, though modernized in form. It is not so much a treatise as a miscellaneous compend of materials relating to agriculture and rural affairs, and it undoubtedly presents the most genuine picture that has been preserved to our time of rustic life in Italy two thousand years ago.

LAELIUS.

Caius Laelius Sapiens, of a distinguished patrician family, was born in Rome, B. C. 186. His surname was given to him for his prudence in retracting certain agrarian measures in which he would have shared with the Gracchi the intensest enmity of the whole patrician body. He was vacillating in his political opinions and proclivities, feeling strong sympathy with the popular cause, yet unwilling to forfeit the friendship and esteem of his own native caste. Though he was not a great man, he filled reputably several high public trusts, both civil and military, and was regarded as the most learned and acute of jurists in augural law, which was largely made up of authority and precedent, and abounded in intricacies and subtilties, while yet it constantly had grave complications with the most important affairs of state.

He was a man of large and varied erudition, was well versed in philosophy, and as a pupil of Diogenes of Babylon, and then of Panaetius, was among the earliest Roman disciples of the Stoic school.

His social qualities won for him many and warm friends. He had an even temper, genial manners, fine conversational powers, ready wit and affluent humor. In the De Senectute he is fitly associated with the younger Scipio Africanus, with whom he lived in the closest intimacy, as his father had with the elder Africanus. Thoroughly amiable in his domestic relations, he seems to have almost anticipated the home life of modern Christendom, and we have accounts of games not unlike our blindman's-buff, in which he and Scipio dropped all dignity and became boys again. Many of his facetious sayings lingered long in the popular memory, and some still survive. The best of them is his reply to an impertinent man, who reproached him with not being worthy of his ancestors, — "But you are worthy of yours."

Of his writings — chiefly orations — nothing remains except a few titles. He was regarded as singularly smooth and elegant in his style; but the Latin tongue was by no means in his day the subtle and flexible organ of thought which Cicero both found and made it, and some of the later grammarians resorted to Laelius for specimens of archaic words and idioms.

SCIPIO.

Publius Cornelius Scipio Aemilianus Africanus Minor was a son of Lucius Aemilius Paullus, and was adopted by his cousin, Publius Cornelius Scipio Africanus, the son of the elder Africanus. He was born in the same year with Laelius. He has his place in history as the most able and successful military commander of his age. He first gained celebrity in Spain as military Tribune under Lucius Lucullus, whom he eclipsed in fame, equally as to courage, integrity, and humanity. At the beginning of the third Punic war he still served as Tribune; but by his valor and skill he so won the suffrages of the army and the confidence of the people, that he was made Consul before the legal age, and was thus placed in supreme command. The war, under his energetic conduct, issued in the capture and destruction of Carthage. He was subsequently chosen Consul a second time, with a view to his service as commander in Spain, where the war had been prolonged for many years, and with repeated disasters for the Roman army. Scipio laid siege to Numantia, and, after the most obstinate resistance on the part of the Spaniards, took the city, levelled it with the ground, reserved fifty of its inhabitants to grace his triumph, and sold the rest of them as slaves.

He was Censor for a year in the interval between his two consulships, and in that office he chose Cato for his model, employed the utmost severity in the repression of extravagance, luxury, and licentiousness, and made some strong and bitter enemies. He was always and consistently an aristocrat, and an opposer of all agrarian measures, and of the self-constituted leaders of the popular or plebeian party; and as his death occurred suddenly and mysteriously, it was supposed that he had been murdered by some one of his political antagonists, probably by Papirius Carbo, who had been unsparing in denunciations and invectives against him as the enemy of the Roman people.

Scipio was one of the most learned and accomplished men of his age, a friend of Polybius and Panaetius, a patron of the poets Lucilius and Terence, and, it was said, — probably on no sufficient evidence, — a collaborator with Terence, or at least a reviser of some of his comedies.

In my translation I have uniformly followed the text of Otto. Few of the various readings are of any importance; and where there is a difference worthy of notice, I find that, so far as I can remember without an exception, Lahmeyer and Sommerbrodt, whose editions I have constantly consulted, coincide with Otto.

CICERO DE SENECTUTE.

I. "Titus, if I can lift or ease the care
That ceaseless burns and rankles in your breast,
What guerdon shall be mine?"
For I may be permitted to address you, Atticus, in the very verses in which Flamininus[1] is addressed by

"That man so rich in probity, not gold,"[2]

although I feel assured that it is by no means true, as of Flamininus, that

"You, Titus, pass but anxious nights and days";

for I know the moderation and evenness of your temperament, and am aware that you brought away from Athens, not only your surname, but also liberal culture and practical wisdom. Yet I am inclined to think that you are sometimes seriously disturbed by the same things1 that weigh heavily on my mind, under which such comfort as may be had is a matter of graver moment, and must be deferred to some other time. But my present purpose is to write to you something about Old Age. For I desire that you and I may be lightened of this burden, which we have in common, of old age already pressing upon us or drawing close at hand,2 though I am certain that you indeed bear and will bear it, as all things else, serenely and wisely. But when it came into my mind to write something about old age, you occurred to me as worthy to receive in this essay an offering of which you and I may in common enjoy the benefit. Indeed, the composition of this book has been so pleasant to me, that it has not only brushed away all the vexations of old age, but has made it even easy and agreeable. In truth, sufficiently worthy praise can never be given to philosophy, whose votaries can pass every period of life without annoyance. But on other philosophical subjects I have said much, and hope to revert to them often; this book, on Old Age, I send specially to you. I put what I have to say, not, like Aristo of Chios,1 into the mouth of Tithonus2 (for a fictitious character cannot speak with authority), but into that of the aged Cato, that the discourse may gain authority from his name. With him I introduce Laelius and Scipio, admiring the ease with which he bears old age, and I give his answers to them. If I make him talk more learnedly than he was wont to do in his books, you may ascribe it to the Greek literature and philosophy, of which, as is well known, he was very studious in his

24

latter years. But what need is there of a longer preface? For, as it were in Cato's own words, you shall forthwith hear all that I think and feel about old age.

II. Scipio. I often express, Marcus Cato, in conversation with Caius Laelius, now present, my admiration of your surpassing and consummate wisdom, in other matters indeed, but especially because I have never perceived that old age was grievous to you, though to old men in general it is so hateful that they account themselves as bearing a burden heavier than Aetna.1

Cato. You seem, Scipio and Laelius, to admire what has been to me by no means difficult. For those who have in themselves no resources for a good and happy life, every period of life is burdensome; but to those who seek all goods from within, nothing which comes in the course of nature can seem evil. Under this head a place especially belongs to old age, which all desire to attain, yet find fault with it when they have reached it. Such is the inconsistency and perverseness of human folly. They say that age creeps upon them faster than they had thought possible. In the first place, who forced them to make this false estimate? In the next place, how could old age be less burdensome to them if it came on their eight-hundredth year than it is in their eightieth? For the time past, however long, when it had elapsed, could furnish no comfort to soothe a foolish old age. If, then, you are wont to admire my wisdom, — would that it were worthy of your appreciation and of my own surname,1 — I am wise in this respect, that I follow and obey Nature, the surest guide, as if she were a god, and it is utterly improbable that she has well arranged the other parts of life, and yet, like an unskilled poet, slighted the last act of the drama. There must, however, of necessity, be some end, and, as in the case of berries on the trees and the fruits of the earth, there must be that which in its season of full ripeness is, so to speak, ready to wither and fall, — which a wise man ought to bear patiently. For to rebel against Nature is but to repeat the war of the Giants with the Gods.

Laelius. Indeed, Cato, you will have rendered us a most welcome service — I will answer for Scipio — if, since we hope, indeed wish, at all events, to become old, we can learn of you, far in advance, in what ways we can most easily bear the encroachment of age.

Cato. I will render this service, Laelius, if, as you say, it will be agreeable to both of you.

Laelius. We do indeed desire, Cato, unless it will give you too much trouble, since you have taken a long journey which we must begin, that you will show us the goal which you have reached.

III. Cato. I will do so, Laelius, to the best of my ability. I have, indeed, often been a listener to complaints of men of my own age, — for, as the old proverb says, "Like best mates with like,"1 — such complaints, for instance, as those which Caius Salinator and Spurius Albinus, men of consular dignity, nearly my coevals, used to make, because they were deprived of the sensual gratifications without which life appeared to them a blank, and because they were neglected by those by whom they were wont to be held in reverence. They seemed to me to lay the blame where it did not belong. For if old age had been at fault, I and all other persons of advanced years would have the same experience; while I have known many old men who have made no complaint, who did not regret their release from the slavery of sensual appetite, and were not despised by their fellow-citizens. But all complaints of this kind are chargeable to character, not to age. Old men who are moderate in their desires, and are neither testy nor morose, find old age endurable; but rudeness and incivility are offensive at any age.

Laelius. You are right, Cato; yet some one may perhaps say that old age seems to you less burdensome on account of your wealth, your large resources, your high rank, but that these advantages fall to the lot of very few.

Cato. There is, indeed, Laelius, something in this; but it by no means gives the full explanation. It is somewhat as in the case of Themistocles in an altercation with a certain native of Seriphos,1 who told him that he owed his illustrious fame, not to his own greatness, but to that of his country; and Themistocles is said to have answered, "If I had been born in Seriphos, I should not have been renowned, nor, by Hercules, would you have been eminent had you been an Athenian." Very much the same may be said about old age, which cannot be easy in extreme poverty, even to a wise man, nor can it be otherwise than burdensome to one destitute of wisdom, even with abundant resources of every kind. The best-fitting defensive armor of old age, Scipio and Laelius, consists in the knowledge and practice of the virtues, which, assiduously cultivated, after the varied experiences of a long life, are wonderfully fruitful, not only because they never take flight, not even at the last moment, — although this is a consideration of prime importance, — but because the consciousness of a well-spent life and a memory rich in good deeds afford supreme happiness.

IV. In my youth I loved Quintus Maximus,1 the one who recovered possession of Tarentum, then an elderly man, as if he had been of my own age; for in him gravity was seasoned by an affable deportment, nor had time made his manners less agreeable. When I first became intimate with him, he was not, indeed, so very old, though advanced in years. I was born the year after his first consulate.2 In my early youth I served as a soldier under him at Capua, and five years afterward at Tarentum. Four years later I was made Quaestor, and held that office in the consulship of Tuditanus and Cethegus, at the time when he, then quite old, urged the passage of the Cincian law concerning gifts and fees.3 He in his age showed in military command all the vigor of youth, and by his perseverance put a check to Hannibal's youthful enthusiasm. My friend Ennius well said of him, —

"One man by slow delays restored our fortunes,
Preferring not the people's praise to safety,
And thus his after-glory shines the more."
How much vigilance, how much wisdom, did he show in the retaking of Tarentum! In my hearing, indeed, when Salinator, who, after the town was taken, had retreated to the citadel, boastfully said, "You recovered Tarentum, Quintus Fabius, by my aid," he replied, laughing, "Very true, for, if you had not lost it, I should never have recovered it."1 Nor had he more eminence as a soldier than he won as a civilian, when, in his second consulate, unsupported by his colleague, Carvilius, he resisted to the utmost of his ability Caius Flaminius, tribune of the people, in his division in equal portions, to the plebeians, of conquered territory in Picenum and Gaul; and when, holding the office of augur, he dared to say that whatever was done for the well-being of the republic was done under the most

28

favorable auspices, but that whatever measures were passed to the injury of the republic were passed under adverse auspices. In him I knew many things worthy of renown, but nothing more admirable than the way in which he bore the death of his son, an illustrious man and of consular dignity. We have in our hands his eulogy on his son, and in reading it we feel that he surpassed in this vein even trained philosophers. Nor was he great only in public and in the eyes of the community; but he was even more excellent in private and domestic life. How rich in conversation! How wise in precept! How ample his knowledge of early times! How thorough his legal science in everything appertaining to his office as an augur!1 He had, too, for a Roman, a large amount of literary culture. He retained in his memory, also, all the details of our wars, whether in Italy or in regions more remote. I indeed availed myself as eagerly of my opportunities of conversing with him as if I had already divined, what proved to be true, that, when he should pass away, no man of equal intelligence and information would be left.

V. To what purpose have I said so much about Maximus? That you may be assured by his example that one has no right to pronounce an old age like his wretched. Yet it is not every one that can be a Scipio or a Maximus, so that he can recall the memory of cities taken, of battles by land and sea, of wars conducted, of triumphs won. There is, however, a calm and serene old age, which belongs to a life passed peacefully, purely, and gracefully, such as we learn was the old age of Plato, who died while writing in his eighty-first year; or that of Isocrates, who says that he wrote the book entitled Panathenaicus1 in his ninety-fourth year, and who lived five years afterwards, and whose preceptor, Leontinus Gorgias, filled out one hundred and seven years without suspending his study and his labor. When he was asked why he was willing to live so long, he replied, "I have no fault to find with old age," — a noble answer, worthy of a learned man. Unwise men, indeed, charge their vices and their faults upon old age. So did not Ennius, of whom I have just spoken, who writes,

"As the brave steed, oft on th' Olympian course Foremost, now worn with years, seeks quiet rest," comparing his own age to that of the brave horse that had been wont to win the race. You can distinctly remember him. The present Consuls, Titus Flamininus and Manius Acilius, were chosen nineteen years after his death, which took place in the consulship of Caepio and the second consulship of Philippus, when I, being sixty-five years old, with a strong voice and sound lungs, spoke in favor of the Voconian law.1 At the age of seventy years — for so many did Ennius live — he bore the two burdens which are esteemed the heaviest, poverty and old age, in such a way that he almost seemed to take delight in them. To enter into particulars, I find on reflection four reasons why old age seems wretched; — one, that it calls us away from the management of affairs; another, that it impairs bodily vigor; the third, that it deprives us to a great degree of sensual gratifications; the fourth, that it brings one to the verge of death. Let us see, if you please, how much force and justice there is in each of these reasons.

VI. Old age cuts one off from the management of affairs. Of what affairs? Of those which are managed in youth and by strength of body? But are there not affairs properly belonging to the later years of life, which may be administered by the mind, even though the body be infirm? Did Quintus Maximus then do nothing? Did Lucius Paullus, your father, Scipio, the father-in-law of that excellent man, my son, do nothing? Did other old men that I might name — the Fabricii, the Curii, the Coruncanii — do nothing, when they defended the republic by their counsel and influence? Blindness came upon Appius Claudius1 in his old age; yet he, when the sentiment of the Senate leaned toward the conclusion of peace and a treaty with Pyrrhus, did not hesitate to say to them what Ennius has fully expressed in verse, —

"Wont to stand firm, upon what devious way
Demented rush ye now?"
and more, most forcibly, to the same purpose. You know the poem, and the speech that Appius actually made is still extant. This took place seventeen years after his second consulship, ten years having intervened between his two consulates, his censorship having preceded the first, — so that you may infer that he was far advanced in age at the time of the war with Pyrrhus, and such is the tradition that has come to us from our fathers. Those, therefore, who deny that old age has any place in the management of affairs, are as unreasonable as those would be who should say that the pilot takes no part in sailing a ship because others climb the masts, others go to and fro in the gangways, others bail the hold, while he sits still in the stern and holds the helm. The old man does not do what the young men do; but he does greater and better things. Great things are accomplished, not by strength, or swiftness, or suppleness of body, but by counsel, influence, deliberate opinion, of which old age is not wont to be bereft, but, on the other hand, to possess them more abundantly. This you will grant, unless I, having been soldier, and military Tribune, and second in command, and as Consul at the head of the army, seem to you now idle

and useless, because I am no longer actively engaged in war. I now prescribe to the Senate what ought to be done, and how. I declare war far in advance against Carthage,1 which has long been plotting to our detriment, and whose hostility I shall never cease to fear, till I know that the city is utterly swept out of being. O that the immortal gods may reserve for you, Scipio, this honor, that you may fully accomplish what your grandfather1 left to be yet done! This is the thirty-third year since his death; but the memory of such a man all coming years will hold in special honor. He died the year before my censorship, nine years after my consulate, during which he was chosen Consul for the second time. If he had lived till his hundredth year, would he have had reason to regret his old age? He would not, indeed, have sought added distinction by running, or leaping, or hurling the spear, or handling the sword, but by counsel, reason, judgment. Unless these were the characteristics of seniors in age, our ancestors would not have called the supreme council the Senate. Among the Lacedaemonians, too, the corresponding name is given to the magistrates of the highest grade, who are really old men.2 But if you see fit to read or hear the history of foreign nations, you will find that states have been undermined by young men, maintained and restored by old men.

"Say, how lost you so great a state so soon?"

For this men ask, as it is asked in Naevius's play of The School, and with other answers this is among the first:
—

"A brood came of new leaders, foolish striplings."

Rashness, indeed, belongs to youth; prudence, to age.

VII. But memory is impaired by age. I have no doubt that it is, in persons who do not exercise their memory, and in those who are naturally slowminded. But Themistocles knew by name all the citizens of Athens, and do you suppose that, at an advanced age, when he met Aristides he called him Lysimachus? I not only know the men who are now living; but I have a clear remembrance of their fathers and their grandfathers. Nor am I afraid to read sepulchral inscriptions, an occupation which is said to destroy the memory;1 on the other hand, my recollection of the dead is thus made more vivid. Then, too, I never heard of an old man's forgetting where he had buried his money. Old men remember everything that they care about,2 — the bonds they have given, what is due to them, what they owe. What shall we say of lawyers? Of priests?1 Of augurs? Of philosophers? How many things do they retain in their memory! Old men have their powers of mind unimpaired, when they do not suspend their usual pursuits and their habits of industry. Nor is this the case only with those in conspicuous stations and in public office; it is equally true in private and retired life. Sophocles in extreme old age still wrote tragedies. Because in his close application he seemed to neglect his property, his sons instituted judicial proceedings to deprive him, as mentally incompetent, of the custody of his estate, in like manner as by our law fathers of families who mismanage their property have its administration taken from them. The old man is said to have then recited to the judges the Oedipus at Colonus, the play which he had in hand and had just written, and to have asked them whether that poem seemed the work of a failing intellect.2 On hearing this, the judges dismissed the case. Did old age then impose silence, in their several modes of utterance, on him, on Homer, on Hesiod, on Simonides, on Stesichorus, on Isocrates and Gorgias of whom I have just spoken, on those foremost of philosophers, Pythagoras and Democritus, on Plato, on Xenocrates, in later time, on Zeno and Cleanthes, or on that Diogenes the Stoic whom you saw when he was in Rome?1 Or with all these men was not activity in their life-work coextensive with their lives? But leaving out of the account these pursuits, which have in them a divine element, I can name old Romans who are farmers in what was the Sabine territory, my neighbors and friends,2 without whose oversight hardly any important work is ever done on their land, whether in sowing, or harvesting, or storing their crops. This, however, is not so surprising in them; for no one is so old that he does not expect to live a year longer. But the same persons bestow great pains in labor from which they know that they shall never derive any benefit.

"He plants
Trees to bear fruit when he shall be no more,"
as our poet Statius says in his Synephebi.3 Nor, indeed can the farmer, though he be an old man, if asked for whom he is planting, hesitate to answer, "For the immortal gods, whose will it was, not only that I should receive this estate from my ancestors, but that I should also transmit it in undiminished value to my posterity."

VIII. What I have just quoted from Caecilius1 about the old man's providing for a coming generation, is very far preferable to what he says elsewhere, —

"Old Age, forsooth, if other ill thou bring not,
This will suffice, that with one's lengthened years
So much he sees he fain would leave unseen," —

34

and much, it may be, that he is glad to see; while youth, too, often encounters what it would willingly shun. Still worse, that same Caecilius writes, —

"The utmost misery of age I count it,
To feel that it is hateful to the young."
Agreeable rather than hateful; for as wise old men are charmed with well-disposed youth, so do young men delight in the counsels of the old, by which they are led to the cultivation of the virtues. I do not feel that I am less agreeable to you than you are to me. — To return to our subject, you see that old age is not listless and inert, but is even laborious, with work and plans of work always in hand, generally, indeed, with employments corresponding to the pursuits of earlier life. But what shall we say of those who even make new acquisitions? Thus we see Solon, in one of his poems, boasting that, as he grows old, he widens the range of his knowledge every day. I have done the like, having learned Greek in my old age, and have taken hold of the study so eagerly — as if to quench a long thirst — that I have already become familiar with the topics from Greek authors which I have been using, as I have talked with you, by way of illustration. When I read that Socrates in his old age learned to play on the lyre, I could have wished to do the same, had the old custom been still rife; but I certainly have worked hard on my Greek.

IX. To pass to the next charge against old age, I do not now desire the bodily strength of youth, any more than when I was a young man I desired the strength of a bull or an elephant. It is becoming to make use of what one has, and whatever you do, to do in proportion to your strength. What language can be more contemptible than that reported of Milon of Crotona,1 when in his old age he saw athletes taking exercise on the race-ground, and is said to have cast his eyes on his own arms, and to have exclaimed, weeping, "But these are dead now"? Not these, indeed, simpleton, so much as you yourself; for you never gained any fame from your own self, but only from your lungs and arms. You hear nothing like this from Sextus Aelius,1 nothing at a much earlier time from Titus Coruncanius,2 nor yet from Publius Crassus,3 who expounded the laws to their fellow-citizens, and whose wisdom grew to their last breath. There is reason, indeed, to fear that a mere orator may lose something of his power with age; for he needs not mind alone, but strong lungs and bodily vigor. Yet there is a certain musical quality of the voice which becomes — I know not how — even more melodious in old age. This, indeed, I have not yet lost, and you see how old I am. But the eloquence that becomes one of advanced years is calm and gentle, and not infrequently a clear-headed old man commands special attention by the simple, quiet elegance of his style. If, however, you cannot attain this merit, you may be able at least to give wholesome advice to Scipio and Laelius. You can at least help others by your counsel; and what is more pleasant than old age surrounded by young disciples? Must we not, indeed, admit that old age has sufficient strength to teach young men, to educate them, to train them for the discharge of every duty? And what can be more worthy of renown than work like this? I used to think Cneius and Publius Scipio, and, Scipio, your two grandfathers, Lucius Aemilius and Publius Africanus, truly fortunate in being surrounded by noble youth; nor are there any masters of liberal culture who are not to be regarded as happy, even though their strength may have failed with lengthened years. This failure of strength, however, is due oftener to the vices of youth than to the necessary infirmity of age; for a licentious and profligate youth transmits to one's later years a worn-out bodily constitution. Cyrus indeed, in his dying speech which Xenophon records, though somewhat advanced in years, says that he has never felt that his old age was more feeble than his youth. I remember in my boyhood Lucius Metellus, who, having been made high-priest four years after his second consulate, served in that office twenty-two years,[1] and was to the very last in such full strength that he did not even feel the loss of youth. There is no need of my speaking of myself, though that is an old man's habit, and is conceded as a privilege of age.

X. Do you not know how very often Homer introduces Nestor as talking largely of his own merits? Nor was there any fear that, while he told the truth about himself, he would incur the reproach of oddity or garrulity; for, as Homer says, "words sweeter than honey flowed from his tongue." For this suavity of utterance he had no need of bodily strength; yet for this alone the leader of the Greeks,[1] while not craving ten like Ajax, says that with ten like Nestor he should be sure of the speedy fall of Troy. — But to return to my own case, I am now in my eighty-fourth year. I should be glad if I could make precisely the same boast with Cyrus; yet, in default of it, I can say this at least, that, while I am not so strong as I was when a soldier in the Punic war, or a Quaestor in the same war, or Consul in Spain, or when, four years afterward, I fought as military Tribune[2] at Thermopylae, in the consulate of Manius Acilius Glabrio, still, as you see, old age has not wholly unstrung my nerves or broken me down. Neither the Senate, nor the rostrum, nor my friends, nor my clients, nor my guests miss the strength that I have lost. Nor did I ever give assent to that ancient and much-lauded proverbial saying, that you must become an old man early if you wish to be an old man long. I should, indeed, prefer a shorter old age to being old before my time. Thus no one has wanted to meet me to whom I have denied myself on the plea of age. Yet I have less strength than either of you. Nor have you indeed the strength of Titus Pontius the centurion.1 Is he therefore any better than you? Provided one husbands his strength, and does not attempt to go beyond it, he will not be hindered in his work by any lack of the requisite strength. It is said that Milo walked the whole length of the Olympian race-ground with a living ox on his shoulders;2 but which would you prefer, — this amount of bodily strength, or the strength of mind that Pythagoras had?3 In fine, I would have you use strength of body while you have it: when it fails, I would not have you complain of its loss, unless you think it fitting for young men to regret their boyhood, or for those who have passed on a little farther in life to want their youth back again. Life has its fixed course, and nature one unvarying way; each age has assigned to it what best suits it, so that the fickleness of boyhood, the sanguine temper of youth, the soberness of riper years, and the maturity of old age, equally have something in harmony with nature, which ought to be made availing in its season. You, Scipio, must have heard what your grandfather's host Masinissa1 does now that he is ninety years old. When he starts on a journey on foot, he never mounts a horse; when he starts on horseback, he never relieves himself by walking; he is never induced by rain or cold to cover his head; he has the utmost power of bodily endurance; and so he performs in full all the offices and functions of a king. Exercise and temperance, then, can preserve even in old age something of one's pristine vigor.

XI. Old age lacks strength, it is said. But strength is not demanded of old age. My period of life is exempted by law and custom from offices which cannot be borne without strength.1 Therefore we are compelled to do, not what we are unable to do, but even less than we can do. Is it said that many old men are so feeble that they are incapable of any duty or charge whatsoever? This, I answer, is not an inability peculiar to old age, but common to bodily infirmity at whatever period of life. How feeble, Scipio, was that son of Africanus who adopted you!2 But for this, he would have shone second in his family as a luminary of the state, adding to his father's greatness a more ample intellectual culture. What wonder, then, is it that old men are sometimes feeble, when it is a misfortune which even the young cannot always escape? Old age, Laelius and Scipio, should be resisted, and its deficiencies should be supplied by faithful effort. Old age, like disease, should be fought against. Care must be bestowed upon the health; moderate exercise must be taken; the food and drink should be sufficient to recruit the strength, and not in such excess as to become oppressive. Nor yet should the body alone be sustained in vigor, but much more the powers of mind; for these too, unless you pour oil into the lamp, are extinguished by old age. Indeed, while overexertion tends by fatigue to weigh down the body, exercise makes the mind elastic. For, when Caecilius speaks of

"Foolish old men, fit sport for comedy,"1

he means those who are credulous, forgetful, weakminded,2 and these are the faults, not of old age, but of lazy, indolent, drowsy old age. As wantonness and licentiousness are the faults of the young rather than of the old, yet not of all young men, but only of

39

such of them as are depraved, so the senile folly which is commonly called dotage3 belongs not to all, but only to frivolous old men. Appius, when both blind and old, governed four grown-up sons, five daughters, a very large household, a numerous body of clients; for he had his mind on the alert, like a bent bow, nor did he, as he became feeble, succumb to old age. He maintained, not only authority, but absolute command over all who belonged to him. His servants feared him; his children held him in awe; all loved him. In that family the manners and discipline of the earlier time were still in the ascendant. Old age, indeed, is worthy of honor only when it defends itself, when it asserts its rights, when it comes into bondage to no one, when even to the last breath it maintains its sway over those of its own family. Still farther, as I hold in high esteem the youth who has in him some of the qualities of age, I have like esteem for the old man in whom there is something of the youth, which he who cultivates may be old in body, but will never be so in mind. I have now in hand the seventh Book of my History.1 I am collecting all the memorials of earlier times. I am just now writing out, as my memory serves me, my speeches in the celebrated cases that I have defended. I am treating of augural, pontifical, civil law. I read a good deal of Greek. At the same time, in order to exercise my memory in the method prescribed by Pythagoras,2 I recall every evening whatever I have said, heard, or done during the day. These are the exercises of the mind; these, the race-ground of the intellect. In these pursuits while I labor vigorously, I hardly feel my loss of bodily strength. I appear in court in behalf of my friends. I often take my place in the Senate, and I there introduce of my own motion1 subjects on which I have thought much and long, and I defend my opinions with strength of mind, not of body. If I were too feeble to pursue this course of life, I still on my bed should find pleasure in thinking out what I could no longer do; but that I am able still to do, as well as to think, is the result of my past life. One who is always occupied in these studies and labors is unaware when age creeps upon him. Thus one grows old gradually and unconsciously, and life is not suddenly extinguished, but closes when by length of time it is burned out.

XII. I come now to the third charge against old age, that, as it is alleged, it lacks the pleasures of sense. O admirable service of old age, if indeed it takes from us what in youth is more harmful than all things else! For I would have you hear, young men, an ancient discourse of Archytas of Tarentum,2 a man of great distinction and celebrity, as it was repeated to me when in my youth I was at Tarentum with Quintus Maximus. "Man has received from nature," said he, "no more fatal scourge than bodily pleasure, by which the passions in their eagerness for gratification are made reckless and are released from all restraint. Hence spring treasons against one's country; hence, overthrows of states; hence, clandestine plottings with enemies. In fine, there is no form of guilt, no atrocity of evil, to the accomplishment of which men are not driven by lust for pleasure. Debaucheries, adulteries, and all enormities of that kind have no other inducing cause than the allurements of pleasure. Still more, while neither Nature nor any god has bestowed upon man aught more noble than mind, nothing is so hostile as pleasure to this divine endowment and gift. Nor while lust bears sway can self-restraint find place, nor under the reign of pleasure can virtue have any foothold whatever." That this might be better understood, Archytas asked his hearers to imagine a person under the excitement of the highest amount of bodily pleasure that could possibly be enjoyed, and maintained that it was perfectly obvious to every one that so long as such enjoyment lasted it was impossible for the mind to act, or for anything to be determined by reason or reflection. Hence he concluded that nothing was so execrable and baneful as pleasure, since, when intense and prolonged, it extinguishes all the light of intellect. That Archytas discoursed thus with Caius Pontius the Samnite, father of the Pontius who defeated the consuls Spurius Postumius and Titus Veturius at the Caudine Forks, I learned from Nearchus of Tarentum, my host, a persistent friend of the Roman people, who said that he had heard it from his elders, Plato having been present when it was uttered, who, I find, came to Tarentum in the consulate of Lucius Camillus and Appius Claudius. To what purpose do I speak thus? That you may understand that, were we indeed unable by reason and wisdom to spurn pleasure, we ought to feel the warmest gratitude to old age for making what is opposed to our duty no longer a source of delight. For pleasure thwarts good counsel, is the enemy of reason, and, if I may so speak, blindfolds the eyes of the mind, nor has it anything in common with virtue. It was, indeed, with great reluctance that, seven years after his consulate, I expelled from the Senate Lucius Flamininus, the brother of that eminently brave man Titus Flamininus; but I thought that such vile conduct as his ought to be branded. For he, during his consulship in Gaul, was persuaded by the companion of his lust, at a banquet, himself to kill with an axe one of the prisoners in chains and under sentence of death.1 He escaped during the censorship of his brother, my immediate predecessor; but I and my colleague Flaccus could not by any possibility give our implied sanction to lust so infamous, so abandoned, which blended with private ignominy disgrace to the office of supreme commander of our army.

XIII. I have often heard from my seniors in age, who said that they when they were boys had so heard from the old men of their time, that Caius Fabricius was wont to express his amazement when, while he was ambassador to King Pyrrhus, Cineas the Thessalonian told him that there was a certain man in Athens,1 professing to be a philosopher, who taught that all that we do ought to be referred to pleasure as a standard. Fabricius having told this to Manius Curius and Titus Coruncanius, they used to wish that the Samnites and Pyrrhus himself might become converts to this doctrine, so that, giving themselves up to pleasure, they might be the more easily conquered. Manius Curius had lived in intimacy with Publius Decius, who, five years before Curius was Consul, had in his fourth consulate devoted his own life for the safety of the state.1 Fabricius had known Publius Decius, Coruncanius had known him, and from that act of self-sacrifice, as well as from his whole life, they inferred that there is that which in its very nature is beautiful and excellent, which is chosen of one's own free will, and which every truly good man pursues, spurning and despising pleasure. But to what purpose am I saying so much about pleasure? Because it is not only no reproach to old age, but even its highest merit, that it does not severely feel the loss of bodily pleasures. But, you may say, it must dispense with sumptuous feasts, and loaded tables, and oft-drained cups. True, but it equally dispenses with sottishness, and indigestion, and troubled dreams.2 But if any license is to be given to pleasure, seeing that we do not easily resist its allurements, — insomuch that Plato calls pleasure the bait of evil, because, forsooth, men are caught by it as fishes by the hook, — old age, while it dispenses with excessive feasting, yet can find delight in moderate conviviality. When I was a boy I often saw Caius Duilius, the son of Marcus, who first gained a naval victory over the Carthaginians, returning home from supper. He took delight in the frequent escort of a torch-bearer and a fluteplayer, — the first person not actually in office who ventured on such display, — a liberty assumed on the score of his military fame.1 But why am I talking about others? I now return to my own case. In the first place, I have for many years belonged to a guild.2 Indeed, guilds were established when I was Quaestor, at the time when the Idaean rites in honor of the Great Mother were adopted in Rome. I then used to feast with my guild fellows, moderately on the whole, yet with something of the joviality that belonged to my earlier years; but with advancing age, day by day, everything is tempered down. Nor did I ever measure my delight at these entertainments by the amount of bodily pleasure more than by the intercourse and conversation of friends. In this feeling, our ancestors fitly called the festive meeting of friends at table, as implying union in life, a convivial meeting, — a much better name than that of the Greeks, who call such an occasion sometimes a compotation, sometimes a social supper,1 evidently attaching the chief importance to that which is of the least moment in an entertainment.

XIV. I, indeed, for the pleasure of conversation, enjoy festive entertainments, even when they begin early and end late,2 and that, not only in the company of my coevals, of whom very few remain, but with those of your age and with you; and I am heartily thankful to my advanced years for increasing my appetency for conversation, and diminishing my craving for food and drink. But if any one takes delight in the mere pleasures of the table, lest I may seem utterly hostile to appetites which perhaps spring from a natural impulse, I would not have it understood that old age is not susceptible of them. I indeed enjoy the ancestral fashion of appointing a master of ceremonies for the feast,1 and the rules for drinking announced from the head of the table, and cups, as in Xenophon's Symposium,2 not over large, and slowly drunk, and the cool breeze for the dining-hall in summer, and the winter's sun or fire.3 Even on my Sabine farm I keep up these customs, and daily fill my table with my neighbors, prolonging our varied talk to the latest possible hour. But it is said that old men have less intensity of sensual enjoyment. So I believe; but there is no craving for it. You do not miss what you do not want. Sophocles very aptly replied, when asked in his old age whether he indulged in sensual pleasure, "May the gods do better for me! I rejoice in my escape from a savage and ferocious tyrant." To those who desire such pleasures it may be offensive and grievous to be debarred from them; but to those already filled and satiated it is more pleasant to lack them than to have them. Though he does not lack who does not want them, I maintain that it is more for one's happiness not to want them. But if young men take special delight in these pleasures, in the first place, they are very paltry sources of enjoyment, and, in the second place, they are not wholly out of the reach of old men, though it be in a restricted measure. As the spectator in the front seat gets the greater enjoyment from the acting of Turpio Ambivius,1 yet those on the farthest seat are delighted to be there; so youth, having a closer view of the pleasures of sense, derives, it may be, more joy from them, while old age has as much enjoyment as it wants in seeing them at a distance. But of what immense worth is it for the soul to be with itself, to live, as the phrase is, with itself, discharged from the service of lust, ambition, strife, enmities, desires of every kind! If one has some provision laid up, as it were, of study and learning, nothing is more enjoyable than the leisure of old age. We saw Caius Gallus, your father's friend, Scipio, almost to the last moment occupied in measuring heaven and earth. How often did the morning light overtake him when he had begun some problem1 by night, and the night when he had begun in the early morning! How did he delight to predict to us far in advance the eclipses of the sun and moon! What pleasure have old men taken in pursuits less recondite, yet demanding keenness and vigor of mind! How did Naevius rejoice in his Punic War!2 Plautus in his Truculentus, — in his Pseudolus!3 I saw also Livius4 in his old age, who, having brought out a play5 six years before I was born, in the consulship of Cento and Tuditanus, continued before the public till I was almost a man. What shall I say of the devotion of Publius Licinius Crassus6 to the study of pontifical and civil law? What of the similar diligence of this Publius Scipio,1 who has just been put at the head of the pontifical college? We have seen all these whom I have named ardently engaged in their old age in their several departments of mental labor. Marcus Cethegus,2 too, whom Ennius rightly called the "Marrow of Persuasion," — how zealously did we see him exercise himself when an old man in the art of speaking! What, then, are the pleasures of feasts, and games, and sensual indulgence, compared with these pleasures? Indeed, it is these intellectual pursuits that for wise and well-nurtured men grow with years, so that it is to Solon's honor that he says, in the verse which I just now quoted, that as he advanced in age he learned something every day, — a pleasure of the mind than which there can be none greater.

XV. I pass now to the pleasures of agriculture, which give me inconceivable delight, to which age is no impediment, and in which one makes the nearest approach to the life of the true philosopher. For the farmer keeps an open account with the earth, which never refuses a draft, nor ever returns what has been committed to it without interest, and if sometimes at a small, generally at an ample rate of increase. Yet I am charmed not only with the revenue, but with the very nature and properties of the soil. When it has received the seed into its softened and prepared bosom, it keeps it buried1 (whence our word for the harrowing2 which buries the seed is derived), then by its pressure and by the moisture which it yields it cleaves the seed and draws out from it the green shoot, which, sustained by its rootlet-fibres, grows till it stands erect on its jointed stalk, enclosed in sheaths, as if to protect the down of its youth, till, emerging from them, it yields the grain, with its orderly arrangement in the ear, defended against predatory birds by its bearded rampart. What can I say of the planting, upspringing, and growth of vines? It is with insatiable delight that I thus make known to you the repose and enjoyment of my old age. Not to speak of the vital power of all things that grow directly from the earth, — which from so tiny a fig or grape seed, or from the very smallest seeds of other fruits or plants, produces such massive trunks and branches, — do not shoots, scions, quicksets, layers, accomplish results which no one can behold without delighted admiration? The vine, indeed, drooping by nature, unless supported, is weighed down to the ground; but to raise itself it embraces with its hand-like tendrils whatever it can lay hold upon; and then, as it twines with multifold and diffusive growth, the art of the vine-dresser trims it close with the pruning-knife, that it may not run unto useless wood and spread too far. Thus in the early spring, in what remains after the pruning, the gem (so called) starts out at the joints of the twigs, from which the incipient cluster of grapes makes its appearance; and this, growing by the moisture of the earth and the heat of the sun, is at first very sour to the taste; then, as it ripens, it becomes sweet, while, clothed with leaves, it lacks not moderate warmth, and at the same time escapes the sun's intenser beams. What can be more gladdening than the fruit of the vine; what more beautiful, as it hangs ungathered? I am charmed, as I have said, not only with the utility of the vine, but equally with the whole process of its cultivation and with its very nature, — with its rows of stakes, the lateral supports from stake to stake, the tying up and training of the vines, the amputation of some of the twigs, of which I have spoken, and the planting of others. What can I tell you of irrigation, and of the repeated digging of the soil to make the ground more fertile? What shall I say of the efficacy of manuring? of which I have written in my book on Farm Life,1 but of which the learned Hesiod, in writing about agriculture, says not a word, — though Homer, who, I think, lived many generations before him, introduces Laertes as relieving his solicitude for his son by tilling and manuring his field. Nor is rural life made cheerful by grainfields, meadows, vineyards, and shrubberies alone, but also by gardens and orchards; then again, by the feeding of sheep, by swarms of bees, by a vast variety of flowers. Nor does one take pleasure merely in the various modes of planting, but equally in those of grafting, than which no agricultural invention shows greater skill.

XVI. I could enumerate many other charms of rural life; but I feel that those which I have named have occupied fully enough of your time. Pardon me; for I am thoroughly versed in everything belonging to country life, and old age is naturally prolix, nor can I pretend to acquit it of all the weaknesses laid to its charge. With your leave I would add, then, that Manius Curius, after winning triumphs over the Samnites, over the Sabines, over Pyrrhus, spent the close of his life in the country; and when I look at his house, which is not far from mine, I cannot sufficiently admire either the self-denying integrity of the man himself or the high moral standard of his time. As Curius was sitting by his hearth the Samnites brought him a large amount of gold, and he spurned the bribe, saying that he thought it better than having gold to bear sway over those who have gold. Such a mind cannot fail to make a happy old age. — But to return to my subject, and not to wander from my own mode of life, there were in those days Senators, that is, as the name implies, old men, living on farms, if indeed Lucius Quinctius Cincinnatus received when ploughing the announcement that he had been made Dictator, under whose dictatorship it was that Caius Servilius Ahala, the Master of Horse, by his order, slew Spurius Maelius, who was aspiring after royalty.1 Curius, too, and other old men, were wont to be summoned from their farms to the Senate, giving thus to the messengers who summoned them a special name2 derived from the highways on which they travelled. Was then the old age of these men who found delight in tilling the ground unhappy? I indeed doubt whether there can be any happier old age, taking into account not only the occupation of agriculture which is healthy for every one, but also the enjoyment of which I have spoken, and the bountiful supply of everything that can be desired for the food of man and the worship of the gods, so that, if any persons have such cravings, we may come again into friendly terms with the pleasures of sense. For a thrifty and industrious farmer has a full wine-cellar, oil-cellar, and larder, and the whole estate is rich, abounding in swine, kids, lambs, fowls, milk, cheese, honey. The farmers themselves are wont to call their garden a second stock of the winter's relishing food.1 All else has the richer zest from the work of leisure time in fowling and hunting. Why should I say more about the green of the meadows, or the rows of trees, or the beauty of the vineyards and the olive groves? To cut the subject short, nothing can be more bountiful for use, or more ornate to the eye, than a well-cultivated farm, to the enjoyment of which advanced years not only interpose no hindrance, but hold forth invitation and allurement; for where can old age find more genial warmth of sunshine or fire, or, on the other hand, more cooling shade or more refreshing waters? Let others take for their own delight arms, horses, spears, clubs, balls, swimming-bouts, and foot-races. From their many diversions let them leave for us old men knuckle-bones and dice.1 Either will serve our turn; but without them old age can hardly be contented.

XVII. Xenophon's books are in many ways very useful, and I beg you to continue to read them. With what a flow of eloquence does he praise agriculture in that book of his about the care of one's estate, called Oeconomicus!2 Still more, to show that there is nothing so worthy of a king as the pursuits of agriculture, he introduces in that book Socrates as telling this story to Critobolus. Cyrus the younger, king of Persia,1 of surpassing genius and renown, when Lysander, the Lacedaemonian, a man of the highest military reputation,2 came to him at Sardis to bring presents from the confederate states, having treated Lysander in other ways with familiar courtesy, showed him an enclosed field planted with the utmost care. Lysander, marvelling at the great height of the trees, their arrangement in ornamental groups,3 the ground thoroughly tilled and free from weeds, and the delicious odors breathing from the flowers, said that he admired, not only the care, but also the skill of him who had planned and laid out these grounds. Cyrus answered, "I myself laid out all this field. The plan is mine; the arrangement is mine, and many of these trees I planted with my own hand." Then Lysander, looking at his purple robe, his elegance of person,4 and his Persian ornaments rich in gold and precious stones, said, "Men may well call you happy, Cyrus, since your fortune corresponds to your merit." This fortune, then, old men can enjoy, nor does age preclude our interest in other things indeed, but least of all in agriculture, to the very last moment of life. We have heard that Marcus Valerius Corvus lived to his hundredth year, passing the close of his life in the country, and engaged to the last in labors of the field. There were forty-six years between his first and his sixth consulship. Thus his term of public life lasted the full number of years which our ancestors accounted as the beginning of old age,1 and his old age was happier than middle life, having more authority with less labor. Indeed, the crowning glory of old age is authority. How great was this in Lucius Caecilius Metellus! How great in Atilius Calatinus! whose eulogy is, —

"Him first of men all tribes and nations own
With one consent."
This, you know, is the inscription on his tomb. He was rightly held, then, in the highest esteem, since all were unanimous in his praise. How great a man did we see in Publius Crassus, the chief priest, of whom I have just spoken, and afterward in Marcus Lepidus, invested with the same priesthood! What shall I say of Paullus or of Africanus? Or of Maximus,2 if I may name him

again? These were men, not only in whose uttered opinion, but in whose very nod, dwelt authority. Old age, especially when it has filled offices of high public trust, has so much authority, that for this alone it is worth all the pleasures of youth.

XVIII. But remember that in all that I say I am praising the old age that has laid its foundations in youth. Hence follows the maxim to which I once gave utterance with the assent of all who heard me: "Wretched is the old age which has to speak in its own defence." White hairs or wrinkles cannot usurp authority; but an early life well spent reaps authority as the fruit of its age. Indeed, attentions which seem trivial and conventional are honorable when merited; for instance, being saluted in the morning, grasped by the hand, received by the rising of those present, escorted to the Forum, escorted home, asked for advice, — customs carefully observed with us, and in other states so far as good manners prevail. It is related that Lysander the Lacedaemonian, of whom I just made mention, used to say that Lacedaemon was the best home for an old man, insomuch as nowhere else was such deference paid to length of years, or age held in such honor. There is, indeed, a tradition that once in Athens, at a public festival, when an old Athenian entered the crowded theatre, no one of his fellow-citizens made room for him, but that, as he approached the place assigned to the delegates from Lacedaemon, they all rose and remained standing till the old man was seated. When they were applauded for this in every possible way by the whole assembly, one of them said, "The Athenians know what is right, but will not do it." Of many excellent usages in our college of Augurs none deserves higher commendation than this, — that the members give their opinions in the order of age, the elder members taking precedence, not only of those who have held higher official rank, but even of those who for the time being are at the head of the state.1 What pleasures of body are then to be compared with the prerogatives of authority? Those who have borne these honors with due dignity seem to me to have thoroughly performed their part in the drama of life, and not, like untrained players, to have broken down in the last act. — But it is said that old men are morose, and uneasy, and irritable, and hard to please; and were we to make the inquiry, we might be told that they are avaricious. But these are faults of character, not of age. Yet moroseness and the faults that I named with it have some excuse, sufficient, not indeed to justify, but to extenuate them. Old men imagine that they are scorned, despised, mocked. Then, too, with a frail body, any cause of vexation is felt more keenly. But such infirmities of temper are corrected by good manners and liberal culture, as we may see in actual life, as well as on the stage in the brothers in the play of the Adelphi. What grimness do we see in one of these brothers; what a genial disposition in the other! So it is in society; for as it is not wine of every vintage, so it is not every temper that grows sour with age. I approve of gravity in old age, so it be not excessive; for moderation in all things is becoming: but for bitterness I have no tolerance. As for senile avarice, I do not understand what it means; for can anything be more foolish than, in proportion as there is less of the way to travel, to seek the more provision for it?

XIX. There remains a fourth reason for deprecating old age, that it is liable to excessive solicitude and distress, because death is so near; and it certainly cannot be very far off. O wretched old man, not to have learned in so long a life that death is to be despised! which manifestly ought to be regarded with indifference if it really puts an end to the soul, or to be even desired if at length it leads the soul where it will be immortal; and certainly there is no third possibility that can be imagined.1 Why then should I fear if after death I shall be either not miserable, or even happy? Moreover, who is so foolish, however young he may be, as to feel sure on any day that he will live till nightfall? Youth has many more chances of death than those of my age. Young men are more liable to illnesses; they are more severely attacked by disease; they are cured with more difficulty. Thus few reach old age. Were it otherwise, affairs would be better and more discreetly managed; for old men have mind and reason and practical wisdom; and if there were none of them, communities could not hold together. But to return to impending death, — can this be urged as a charge against old age, when you see that it belongs to it in common with youth? I felt in the death of my most excellent son,1 and equally, Scipio, in that of your brothers,2 who were born to the expectation of the highest honors, that death is common to all ages. But, it is said, the young man hopes to live long, while the old man can have no such hope. The hope, at any rate, is unwise; for what is more foolish than to take things uncertain for certain, false for true? Is it urged that the old man has absolutely nothing to hope? For that very reason he is in a better condition than the young man, because what the youth hopes he has already obtained. The one wishes to live long; the other has lived long. Yet, ye good gods, what is there in man's life that is long? Grant the very latest term of life; suppose that we expect to reach the age of the king of Tartessus.1 For it is on record that a certain Arganthonius, who reigned eighty years in Gades, lived to the age of a hundred and twenty. But to me no life seems long that has any end. For when the end comes, then that which has passed has flowed away; that alone remains which you have won by virtue and by a good life. Hours, indeed, and days, and months, and years, glide by, nor does the past ever return, nor yet can it be known what is to come. Each one should be content with such time as it is allotted to him to live. In order to give pleasure to the audience, the actor need not finish the play; he may win approval in whatever act he takes part in; nor need the wise man remain on the stage till the closing plaudit. A brief time is long enough to live well and honorably;1 but if you live on, you have no more reason to mourn over your advancing years, than the farmers have, when the sweet days of spring are past, to lament the coming of summer and of autumn. Spring typifies youth, and shows the fruit that will be; the rest of life is fitted for reaping and gathering the fruit. Moreover, the fruit of old age is, as I have often said, the memory and abundance of goods previously obtained. But all things that occur according to nature are to be reckoned as goods; and what is so fully according to nature as for old men to die? while the same thing happens to the young with the opposition and repugnancy of nature. Thus young men seem to me to die as when a fierce flame is extinguished by a stream of water; while old men die as when a spent fire goes out of its own accord, without force employed to quench it. Or, as apples, if unripe, are violently wrenched from the tree, while, mature and ripened, they fall, so force takes life from the young, maturity from the old; and this ripeness of old age is to me so pleasant, that, in proportion as I draw near to death, I seem to see land, and after a long voyage to be on the point of entering the harbor.

XX. The close of other ages is definitely fixed;1 but old age has no fixed term, and one may fitly live in it so long as he can observe and discharge the duties of his station, and yet despise death. Old age, fearless of death, may transcend youth in courage and in fortitude. Such is the meaning of Solon's answer to the tyrant Pisistratus, who asked him what was his ground of confidence in resisting him so boldly, and Solon replied, "Old age." But the most desirable end of life is when — the understanding and the other faculties unimpaired — Nature, who put together, takes apart her own work. As he who built a ship or a house can take it to pieces the most easily, so Nature, who compacted the human frame, is the best agent for its dissolution. Then, again, whatever has been recently put together is torn apart with difficulty; old fabrics, easily. Thus what brief remainder there may be of life ought to be neither greedily sought by old men, nor yet abandoned without cause,2 and Pythagoras forbids one to desert the garrison and post of life without the order of the commander, that is, God. There are extant, indeed, verses of Solon the Wise,1 in which he says that he does not want to die without the grief and lamentation of his friends, desiring, as I suppose, to be held dear by those in intimate relation with him; but I am inclined to prefer what Ennius writes, —

"Let no one honor me with tears, or make
A lamentation at my funeral."
He thinks that death is not to be mourned, since it is followed by immortality. There may be, indeed, some painful sensation in dying, yet for only a little while, especially for the old; after death there is either desirable sensation or none at all. But such thoughts as this ought to be familiar to us from youth, that we may make no account of death. Without such habits of thought one cannot be of a tranquil mind; for it is certain that we must die, and it is uncertain whether it be not this very passing day. How then can one be composed in mind while he fears death, which impends

over him every hour? On this subject there seems no need of a long discussion, when I recall to memory, — not Lucius Brutus, who was slain in setting his country free; not the two Decii, spurring their horses to a death of their own choice; not Marcus Atilius, returning to the punishment of death that he might keep faith with an enemy; not the two Scipios, who wanted to block the way for the Carthaginians even with their own bodies; not your grandfather, Lucius Paullus, who yielded up his life to expiate his colleague's rashness in the ignominious battle of Cannae; not Marcus Marcellus, whose body not even the most cruel of enemies would suffer to lack the honor of a funeral,1 — but our legions, often going, as I have said in my History,2 with a firm and cheerful mind, to scenes of peril whence they expected never to return. Shall well-trained old men, then, fear what youth, and they not only untrained, but even fresh from the country, despise? — In fine, satiety of life, as it seems to me, creates satiety of pursuits of every kind. There are certain pursuits belonging to boyhood; do grownup young men therefore long for them? There are others appertaining to early youth; are they required in the sedate period of life which we call middle age? This, too, has its own pursuits, and they are not sought in old age. As the pursuits of earlier periods of life fail, so in like manner do those of old age. When this period is reached, satiety of life brings a season ripe for death.

XXI. I see, indeed, no reason why I should hesitate to tell you how I myself feel about death; for I seem to have a clearer view of it, the nearer I approach it. My belief is that your father, Publius Scipio, and yours, Caius Laelius, men of the highest renown and my very dear friends, are living, and are living the only life that truly deserves to be called life. Indeed, while we are shut up in this prison of the body, we are performing a heavy task laid upon us by necessity; for the soul, of celestial birth, is forced down from its supremely high abode, and, as it were, plunged into the earth, a place uncongenial with its divine nature and its eternity. I believe, indeed, that the gods disseminated souls, and planted them in human bodies, that there might be those who should hold the earth in charge, and contemplating the order of celestial beings, should copy it in symmetry and harmony of life. I was led to this belief, not only by reason and argument, but by the pre-eminent authority of the greatest philosophers. I learned that Pythagoras and the Pythagoreans, almost our fellow-countrymen,1 who used to be called Italian philosophers, never doubted that we had souls that emanated from the universal divine mind. I was impressed, also, by what Socrates, whom the oracle of Apollo pronounced the wisest of men, taught with regard to the immortality of souls, on the last day of his life. Why should I say more? So have I convinced myself, so I feel, that since such is the rapid movement of souls, such their memory of the past and foresight of the future, so many are the arts, so profound the sciences, so numerous the inventions to which they have given birth, the nature which contains all these things cannot be mortal; that as the soul is always active, and has no prime cause of motion inasmuch as it puts itself in motion, so it can have no end of motion, because it can never abandon itself; moreover, that since the nature of the soul is uncompounded, and has in itself no admixture of aught that is unequal to or unlike itself, it is indivisible, and if so, is imperishable; and that there is strong reason for believing that men know a great deal before they are born in the ease with which boys learn difficult arts, and the rapidity with which they seize upon innumerable things, so that they seem not to be receiving them for the first time, but to be recalling and remembering them. This is the sum of what I have from Plato.1

XXII. In Xenophon's narrative,2 the elder Cyrus says in dying: "Do not imagine, my beloved sons, that when I go from you I shall be nowhere, or shall cease to be. For while I was with you, you did not see my soul; but you inferred its existence from the things which I did in this body. Believe then that I am the same being, even though you do not see me at all. The fame of illustrious men would not remain after their death, if the souls of those men did nothing to perpetuate their memory. Indeed, I never could be persuaded that souls live while they are in mortal bodies and die when they depart from them, nor yet that the soul becomes void of wisdom on leaving a senseless body; but I have believed that when, freed from all corporeal mixture, it begins to be pure and entire, it then is wise. Moreover, when the constitution of man is dissolved by death, it is obvious what becomes of each of the other parts; for they all go whence they came: but the soul alone is invisible, alike when it is present in the body and when it departs. You see nothing so nearly resembling death as sleep. Now in sleep souls most clearly show their divineness;1 for when they are thus relaxed and free, they foresee the future. From this we may understand what they will be when they have entirely released themselves from the bonds of the body. Therefore, if these things are so, reverence me as a divine being.2 If, however, the soul is going to perish with the body, you still, revering the gods who protect and govern all this beautiful universe, will keep my memory in pious and inviolate regard."1

XXIII. Such were the last words of Cyrus. Let me now, if it seem good to you, express my own opinion and feeling. No one will ever convince me, Scipio, that your father Paullus, or your two grandfathers, Paullus and Africanus, or the father or the uncle of Africanus, or many men of surpassing excellence whom I need not name, undertook such noble enterprises which were to belong to the grateful remembrance of posterity, without a clear perception that posterity belonged to them. Or think you, — if after the manner of old men I may boast a little on my own account, — think you that I would have taken upon myself such a vast amount of labor, by day and by night, at home and in military service, if I had been going to put the same limits to my fame that belong to my earthly life? Would it not have been much better to pass my time in leisure and quiet, remote from toil and strife? But somehow my soul, raising itself2 above the present, was always looking onward to posterity, as if, when it departed from life, then at length it would truly live. But unless souls were indeed immortal, men's souls would not strive for undying fame in proportion to their transcending merit. What? Since men of the highest wisdom die with perfect calmness, those who are the most foolish with extreme disquiet, can you doubt that the soul which sees more and farther perceives that it is going to a better state, while the soul of obtuser vision has no view beyond death? For my part, I am transported with desire to see your fathers whom I revered and loved; nor yet do I long to meet those only whom I have known, but also those of whom I have heard and read, and about whom I myself have written. Therefore one could not easily turn me back on my lifeway, nor would I willingly, like Pelias,1 be plunged in the rejuvenating caldron. Indeed, were any god to grant that from my present age I might go back to boyhood, or become a crying child in the cradle, I should steadfastly refuse; nor would I be willing, as from a finished race, to be summoned back from the goal to the starting-point. For what advantage is there in life? Or rather, what is there of arduous toil that is wanting to it? But grant all that you may in its favor, it still certainly has either its excess or its fit measure of duration. I am not, indeed, inclined to speak ill of life, as many and even wise men have often done, nor am I sorry to have lived; for I have so lived that I do not think that I was born to no purpose. Yet I depart from life, as from an inn, not as from a home; for nature has given us here a lodging for a sojourn, not a place of habitation. O glorious day, when I shall go to that divine company and assembly of souls, and when I shall depart from this crowd and tumult! I shall go, not only to the men of whom I have already spoken, but also to my Cato, than whom no better man was ever born, nor one who surpassed him in filial piety, whose funeral pile I lighted, — the office which he should have performed for me, — but whose soul, not leaving me, but looking back upon me, has certainly gone into those regions whither he saw that I should come to him. This my calamity I seemed to bear bravely. Not that I endured it with an untroubled mind; but I was consoled by the thought that there would be between us no long parting of the way and divided life. For these reasons, Scipio, as you have said that you and Laelius have observed with wonder, old age sits lightly upon me. Not only is it not burdensome; it is even pleasant. But if I err in believing that the souls of men are immortal, I am glad thus to err, nor am I willing that this error in which I delight shall be wrested from me so long as I live; while if in death, as some paltry philosophers1 think, I shall have no consciousness, the dead philosophers cannot ridicule this delusion of mine. But if we are not going to be immortal, it is yet desirable for man to cease living in his due time; for nature has its measure, as of all other things, so of life. Old age is the closing act of life, as of a drama, and we ought in this to avoid utter weariness, especially if the act has been prolonged beyond its due length. — I had these things to say about old age, which I earnestly hope that you may reach, so that you can verify by experience what you have heard from me.

Printed in Great Britain
by Amazon

40642395R10037